# The Cat That
# SCRATCHED

For Dad and in memory of Creature J.L.
To Sarah Stoffer K.P.

A Red Fox Book

Published by Random House Children's Books
20 Vauxhall Bridge Road, London SW1V 2SA

A division of Random House UK Ltd
London Melbourne Sydney Auckland
Johannesburg and agencies throughout the world

Copyright © text Jonathan Long 1994
Copyright © illustrations Korky Paul 1994

1 3 5 7 9 10 8 6 4 2

First published in Great Britain by
The Bodley Head Children's Books 1994

Red Fox edition 1997

Printed in China

RANDOM HOUSE UK Limited Reg. No. 954009

ISBN 0 09 935371 7

# The Cat That SCRATCHED

### Jonathan Long and Korky Paul

SCRATCH SCRITCH SCRATCH SCRATCH SCRATCH SCRITCH SCRITCH SCRATCH SCRATCH SCRATCH SCRATCH SCRITCH SCRATCH SCRITCH SCRATCH SCRATCH

**RED FOX**

There once was a cat with a terrible itch.
She had a flea in her fur which was making her twitch.

She scratched herself here and she scritched herself there.
She scritched upside down and she scratched in mid air.

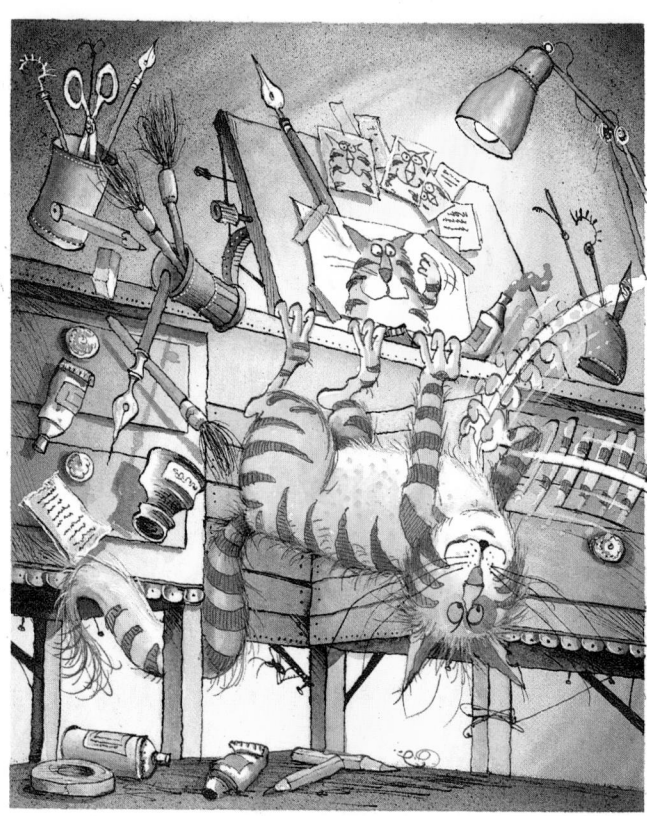

She whirled her paws fast and she span like a top,
Then fell head over heels and she rolled to a stop.

'Ha ha ha,' said a voice, all tiny and teasy.
'To get rid of me won't be nearly that easy.'

'You talkative tickle,' said the cat. 'You bothersome bug!'
'When I've finished with you, you won't sound so smug.'

SCRITCH
SCRATCH SCRATCH
SCRITCH SCRATCH SCRAT
SCRITCH
SCRATCH SCRATCH
SCRATCH

So she went to the cupboard in one of the rooms
And found a big hoover amongst all the brooms.

She plugged in the plug and she flicked on the switch,
And said, 'Say your prayers, you tortuous titch.'

She hoovered her tum and her ears and her nose,
And each one of her legs right down to her toes.

But catastrophe struck – her tail was sucked in,
And the hoover exploded with a deafening din!

When she opened her eyes, she was flat on the ceiling.
An unusual position which was most unappealing.

'Ha ha ha,' said a voice, all tiny and teasy.
'To get rid of me won't be nearly that easy.'

'You nigglesome nit!' said the cat. 'You mischievous mite!
I'm really mad now so get set for a fight.'

So she ran down the road to a friendly hairdresser
Who wore a pink gown and was called Trendy Tessa.

'Listen Tess,' said the cat. 'Keep this hush-hush,
There's an itch in my fur and I need a good brush.'

So Tess combed her all over with a big spiky comb,
And curled her and clipped her and sprayed her with foam.

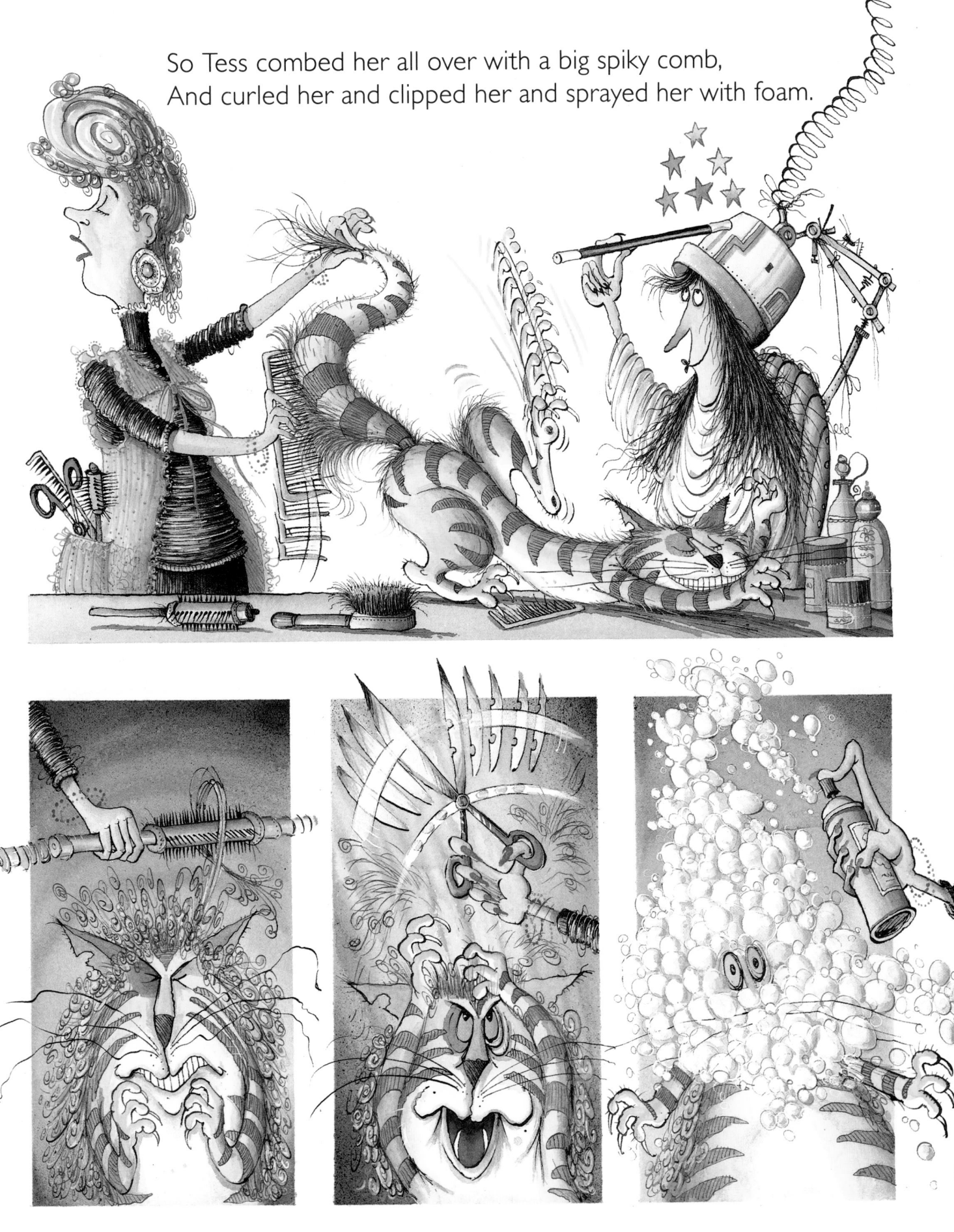

But when it was done, the poor cat looked a fright,
And can you believe it – she felt a small bite!

'Ha ha ha,' came a voice, all tiny and teasy.
'To get rid of me won't be nearly that easy.'

'You loudmouthed louse!' said the cat. 'You pernickety pest!
I'm going to put you to the ultimate test.'

SCRATCH SCRITCH
SCRITCH SCRATCH SCRITCH
SCRITCH SCRITCH SCRITCH
SCRATCH SCRATCH
SCRATCH
SCRATC!
SCRATCH

So she went to a carwash and paid 50p,
To a fat man in jeans who was drinking some tea.

Then she dived right inside a very large washer,
Which had rollers and soapers and a powerful splosher.

Scruba-dub-dub, it went, duba-scrub-scrub,
And rolled her around like a sock in a tub.

But she swallowed some water which made her all soggy,
And she had to leap out; a water-logged moggy.

'Ha ha ha,' came a voice, all tiny and teasy.
'To get rid of me won't be nearly that easy.'

'Oh dear,' wailed the cat, feeling awfully poorly,
'It looks like I'm stuck with this darned creepy-crawly.'

SCRATCH SCRITCH
SCRITCH SCRATCH
SCRATCH
SCRITCH SCRATCH
SCRITCH SCRATCH
SCRATCH SCRATC
SCRATCH SCRATC
SCRATC
SCRITCH

But just then she heard shouts and a hullaballoo:
Her cousin the lion had escaped from the zoo.

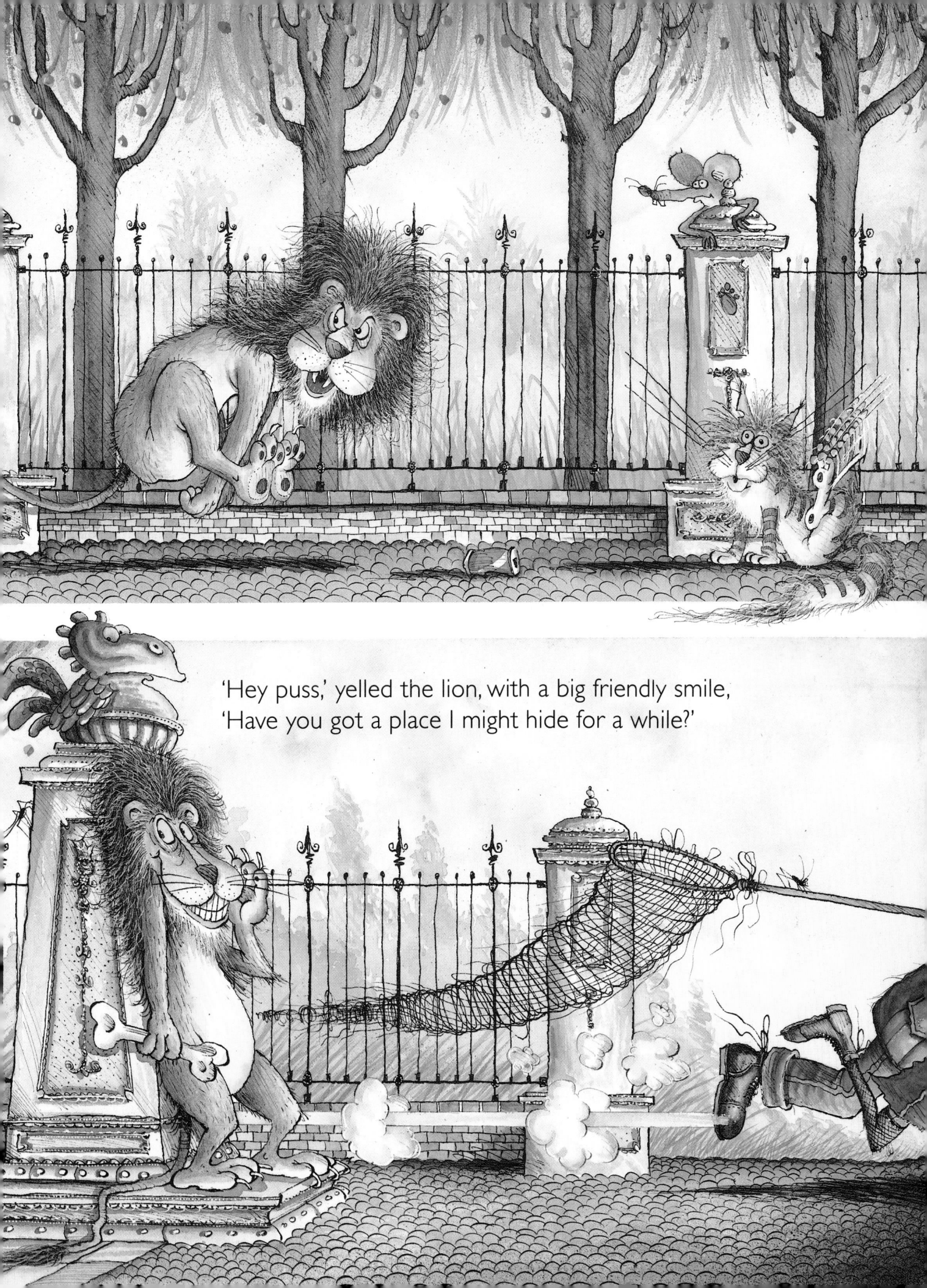

'Hey puss,' yelled the lion, with a big friendly smile,
'Have you got a place I might hide for a while?'

But before she could answer they heard a small pop,
The flea had moved house with a seven yard hop.

But with an elegant hitch the lion lifted its paw,
Flicked out the flea and squashed it flat on the floor.

'Grrr,' said the lion, 'that flea didn't half bungle.
Nobody messes with the King Of The Jungle.'

'Silly me,' said the cat, 'no one needs tricks.
Just trust your family if you're in a fix.'

So she invited him home, and they put up a sign,
Which spelled out in big letters:

BEWARE
OF THE
LION

Then they fell fast asleep with their tails all curled,
The two happiest cats you could meet in the world.

# Some bestselling Red Fox picture books

THE BIG ALFIE AND ANNIE ROSE STORYBOOK
*by Shirley Hughes*
OLD BEAR
*by Jane Hissey*
OI! GET OFF OUR TRAIN
*by John Burningham*
DON'T DO THAT!
*by Tony Ross*
NOT NOW, BERNARD
*by David McKee*
ALL JOIN IN
*by Quentin Blake*
THE WHALES' SONG
*by Gary Blythe and Dyan Sheldon*
JESUS' CHRISTMAS PARTY
*by Nicholas Allan*
THE PATCHWORK CAT
*by Nicola Bayley and William Mayne*
MATILDA
*by Hilaire Belloc and Posy Simmonds*
WILLY AND HUGH
*by Anthony Browne*
THE WINTER HEDGEHOG
*by Ann and Reg Cartwright*
A DARK, DARK TALE
*by Ruth Brown*
HARRY, THE DIRTY DOG
*by Gene Zion and Margaret Bloy Graham*
DR XARGLE'S BOOK OF EARTHLETS
*by Jeanne Willis and Tony Ross*
WHERE'S THE BABY?
*by Pat Hutchins*